ISBN-10: 1480241377

ISBN-13: 978-1480241374

To receive FREE Templates of Recommendation Letters, or for inquiries, send your purchase receipt to:

reza@effortlessMath.com

CONTENTS

INTRODUCTION

At top universities and colleges, the competition among candidates is fierce. Therefore, the quality of a candidate's application plays the key role. In this regard, the letter of recommendation is one of the most essential aspects of a student's graduate school application. Powerful letters of recommendation is the crucial factor in whether a student can be admitted into a graduate program. Therefore, writing a recommendation letter is a huge responsibility and should be taken seriously.

Sometimes, it is helpful to look at sample letters of recommendation to see exactly how they should look and to become more familiar with the content, tone, and style of an influential recommendation letter.

This book offers 100 sample letters of recommendation for master and PhD candidates. The sample letters are provided by university and college professors for their students, with various academic backgrounds. These letters helped the candidates gain admittance into their desire programs in esteemed universities around the world.

If you're a graduate candidate, examples of strong letters of recommendation can help you understand how to get the best letters yourself from your teachers. If you're a college professor, the examples in this book will inspire you to support your students strongly as they apply to graduate programs.

WHAT IS A LETTER OF RECOMMENDATION?

A letter of recommendation is a letter of reference in which the writer evaluates the qualities and capabilities of the person being recommended. The writer recommends the person in terms of his ability to perform a certain task. This recommendation letter reflects on how well the individual will shine in the area he/ she is applying for; and the capabilities he/ she hold.

In order to get an admission in a masters or Ph.D. program, a letter of recommendation is important. It is an essential part of college applications. The basic purpose of the letter of recommendation is to give the admission committees information. The information provided is related to the academic and work accomplishments of the candidate. It states reasons why the admission committee should recognize the applicant's achievements and character.

Different universities require different number of recommendation letters. Some demand one while some may require the applicants to submit at least 3 letters of recommendation. These may come from the professors, employers, or the public figures who know the abilities of the applicant.

WHY ARE RECOMMENDATION LETTERS IMPORTANT?

In universities, the admission committee members are way too busy to evaluate each candidate based on education and experiences. They cannot meet each and every student to evaluate them personally. This is when the recommendation letters, along with the candidate's own personal essay, play a vital role in illuminating the candidate's intellectual and personal qualities.

A letter of recommendation portrays all the traits of the candidate and best explains the skills that make the candidate different. Evaluators want to observe how well individuals talk about their work ethic, experience, intelligence and personality.

It also has become a standard practice that universities offering masters and Ph.D. programs require the candidates to submit at least two to three recommendation letters. A modest university will request the candidate to submit at least one letter from a professor, one letter from an employer, and one letter from another individual who has experience evaluating your academics or work experience. Candidates can also use predesigned templates of recommendation letters offered by some universities.

THE CONTENTS OF A LETTER OF RECOMMENDATION

Every recommendation letter should include three components.

- A paragraph that explains how you know the applicant and the duration of your relationship with them.
- An evaluation of the applicant and their skills and accomplishments.
- And finally a summary that explains why you would recommend this applicant and to what degree you would recommend her/him.

Below are some areas to consider when writing a powerful recommendation letter.

Adopt honesty and positivity

Use personal stories or observations about your work experiences with the applicant. Of course, objective facts are important, but they must be balanced with personal reflections about the candidate. Do not over exaggerate about the qualities but also do not sound too low. Adopting a balanced approach can be very helpful.

Mention the qualities

In a letter of recommendation, you should mention the qualities of the applicant that match with the criteria of the masters or Ph.D. program. Admission departments look for "X factors" rather scores or grades and these qualities impress them most. The writer should also mention the duration of his association with the applicant.

Nature of association with the applicant

In a letter of recommendation, the nature of the association with the applicant should be mentioned. The writer should explain how he knows the applicant so that the university staff is clear about the relationship of the writer and the applicant. If you are an employee, peer, colleague or a friend, you should mention it in the letter.

How the applicant fits in the criteria

evaluators assess the students based on the set criteria for the program. A letter of recommendation should suggest the admission department how the applicant fits in the prescribed criteria for the program. Even if it is a masters or a Ph.D. program, there is a criteria that the applicants need to fulfil in order to get admission in the university.

Write about the willingness

A letter of recommendation should also contain the need and willingness of the candidate to get admission in the university. You cannot recommend a certain person if he/ she is not willing to undertake a program.

These are some of the main components that should be included in the letter of recommendations. These components play a vital role in the assessment of the applications. The letters having these points are highly likely to be accepted. It is also worth noticing that a letter of recommendation is like a person himself is recommending a person, so the credibility is at stake. Therefore, the best approach to write an effective letter is by including all these components while being concise and profession which is the key.

TIPS FOR WRITING A WINNING RECOMMENDATION LETTER

Writing a recommendation letter isn't always easy. You should be honest and convey the student's best characteristics and qualities without making it read like a template.

Here are some tips for writing a perfect recommendation letter:

Always be selective

Before you recommend someone, you should make sure that you know the person quite well. Programs that require Letters of recommendation assume that you know the person and have worked with the applicant. Your credibility is at stake when writing a recommendation letter. If you do not know the applicant, you cannot be 100% certain about the capabilities of the person therefore cannot recommend with complete authority. If you know the applicant, you should not hesitate in writing one.

Be relevant

A letter of recommendation is a straight forward letter. It should contain all the relevant details about the applicant. You should ask the applicant for the details so you may incorporate them in your letter. Even if you know the applicant, there can be some skills or reasons you may not be aware of. That is why it is recommended to consult the applicant before writing the recommendation letter.

Write the best qualities

Admission departments receive tons of applications each day with recommendation letters. So what exactly are they looking for? Answer is very simple, beyond education and experience they are looking for traits that outshine the other applicants. You should pinpoint those characteristics and accomplishments which you feel can make the applicant different from the rest.

Maintain a professional tone

Tone is a component of the letter of recommendation. It depicts the writer's authority and therefore it should have a professional tone besides being concise and readable. A recommendation letter is different to an informal letter. You cannot use frank and open words. In order to make your letter captivating, try to use professional terms that relate to the candidate's competence. Using fancy words will make your recommendation a part of the crowd.

Short and simple

Conciseness is the key. The department's staff are too busy to read each and every letter. You should make sure that your letter is short and sweet yet professional. What you can do is try using the 7 C's like that in business management. It will make your letter of recommendation professional and acceptable. Make sure that the letter is not more than one single page or maximum two pages.

DOS AND DON'TS FOR WRITING A PERSUASIVE LETTER OF RECOMMENDATION

This list of dos and don'ts will help you write a persuasive and effective recommendation letter.

What to Do?

- The applicant must select a referee who knows them well. The referee must know about the academic and professional achievements of the applicants.
- Ask for a recommendation in person instead of sending an email.
- Letter of recommendation should be written by a referee that knows the applicant well.
- It is better to find a referee beforehand rather than rushing at the eleventh hour. The recommendation letter might do more harm than good.
- The referee must know all requirements of the letter of recommendation and the deadline as well.
- It is imperative to state the truth in the letter.
- Assist the referee by providing any information to be included in the letter of recommendation.

- The referee must be specific and state examples of the applicant's achievements and qualities.
- Applicant should provide sufficient time to the referee to write the letter of recommendation.
- If there is any achievement of the applicant related to the course they wish to study, should be mentioned.
- Every information mentioned in the letter must match with the applicant's academic scores.
- The recommendation letter should be sent well before the deadline date.
- Ensure you have a copy of the letter as a backup option.
- Make sure that your letter is no more than a single page, as a reviewer will have many recommendation letters.
- Send a thank you note to the referee.

What Not to Do?

- The applicant should not be hesitant to get as many as recommendation letter as possible. The applicant can choose the letter that recommends them the best.
- Do not ask someone to lie and avoid fabricating tales in the letter.

- The letter of recommendation must not be in conflict with the rest of the application. It should not be a copy of it either.

- It is illegal to write the letter themselves and put someone else's signature. The applicant must not do this.

- Do not use vague words like hardworking or good.

- The letter must be a recommendation, not a bragging session.

- If it is the requirement of the institution that applicant must not read the letter. Then the applicant should not receive the letter.

- The letter must not contain spelling or grammatical errors.

- Do not forget to thank the referee.

To help you learn more about the content, tone, and style of an influential recommendation letter, I have prepared 100 sample recommendation letters. The sample letters (with modifications and deletions in order to preserve anonymity) are provided by university and college professors for their students, with various academic backgrounds. These letters helped the candidates gain admittance into their desire programs in esteemed universities around the world.

If you're a graduate candidate, examples of strong letters of recommendation can help you understand how to get the best letters yourself from your teachers. If you're a college professor, the examples in this book will inspire you to support your students strongly as they apply to graduate programs.

1

To whom it may concern:

I am writing this letter of recommendation in support of Mr. Paul Miller to attend your university for the graduate program in Electronics Engineering. I have known him for more than two years as a student in the electrical and computer engineering department, University of xxx.

Paul has taken several courses with me in Electronics area. In all these courses, he showed outstanding performance in every assumed task, which resulted in his excellent grades. A major part of each course was research projects. Paul's superb accomplishment in these projects demonstrated his ability for research activity to me. Considering his performance in these courses, I have found Paul to be a smart, diligent, and innovative student. He is able to use all his knowledge and intelligence to solve the problems he faces.

In addition to what I know about him from our direct interaction through these courses, I am aware that he has reached unique achievements in other courses and this is clear from his grades. His high GPA ranks him first among his classmates.

Generally, I have found Paul to be an intelligent student capable of cooperating in a research team. He is a highly motivated student who can offer good solutions for challenging problems and conduct his research with minimal guidance. In addition, Paul is very sincere and orderly with a friendly personality.

Given his talents and interests, I believe that he will have a successful graduate education once he is given the chance. Therefore, I would like to take this opportunity to recommend this talented student for admission in your graduate program without any reservation.

Sincerely,

Prof. Kevin Right

Email:

Phone:

2

To whom it may concern:

I wish to record my esteem for Max Bush. My first contact with Max was during the fall of 2009, when he was my student in a course entitled "Introduction to Management Research Methods". There were more than 65 talented students in the class. However, Max managed to earn the highest grade on both the midterm and final exam. This is a reliable indicative of his capabilities.

At the beginning of the spring semester of 2010, he volunteered to become my teaching assistant for the IT Management course. I explained to him that it would be a demanding task because of the large number of students in the class, and it is a big responsibility, because this is an important course in the students' academic careers. Despite these obstacles, he was still determined to take on the challenge. His responsibilities included giving and grading quizzes, helping students solve problems, and grading their exercises. Max's great self-confidence and good rapport with the students really set him apart from other teaching assistants I had worked with in the past. He is particularly gifted at identifying students' needs and encouraging their contributions.

I have no doubt that Max's experiences during last two years, and his enthusiasm and exceptional abilities, will lead him to be a great teacher in the future. His warm and sincere nature has made it a pleasure to work with him. Therefore, I would like to strongly recommend him for admission to your graduate program. If you would like further elaboration, please feel free to contact me.

Sincerely yours,

Professor David Payne

Professor of Management Department at Nagoya University

3

To whom it may concern:

It gives me immense satisfaction to recommend a beloved and remarkable student, Joe Lee, for admission to your graduate program and write this letter on his behalf. As his research advisor, I have worked closely with him for about two years in the coating laboratory and feel that he is a deserving candidate for your graduate program.

During his presence here, Joe has always displayed a noticeable work ethic and a devotion to success. He has demonstrated enthusiasm and analytical talent for research and graduate study. His research endeavors have led to pleasing results including several conference and journal papers.

Joe is a bright and perceptive individual with a strong character. With his tenacity and hard work, I am confident that he will succeed in all his efforts. In addition, he is exceptionally cooperative. He owns the capability to contribute effectively as a part of a team and as a team leader. Because of his social abilities, many students seek his guidance and suggestions and find his eagerness and ardor inspiring. In fact, he enjoys helping other people and desires to make a positive contribution to the accomplishments of his friends.

As indicated by his background, Joe has a marvelous organizational capability and is able handle various duties with satisfactory results in spite of time limits.

In closing, it is with sincere conviction that I enthusiastically recommend Joe as a candidate for the graduate program at your university. If you have further questions regarding Joe or this recommendation, please do not hesitate to contact me.

Sincerely,

Prof. Jack Williams, Ph.D.

4

Letter of Recommendation for Anna Clark

Prof. David White

01/22/2011

Dear Colleagues

I consider it a great opportunity to recommend Miss Anna Clark. She is a worthy candidate for your advanced program in Organizational Behavior. I am a senior professor specializing in the field of Accounting for over 30 years. As a professor at the department of Management and Business Studies, I have a close understanding of Anna's academic capability.

Anna enrolled into our department with a notable entrance score. She has gained significant academic success during her college years. In fact, her ranking among her classmates, both as an undergraduate student and as a graduate student, is a good indication of her high potentials and capabilities.

I have also discovered her to be perseverant and enthusiastic in studies and extracurricular activities. Anna is an active member of the Student Association in our department. She was also selected by students as their representative at xxx conference last year. During the time I have known Anna, I have been deeply impressed by her capabilities of organization and her sense of involvement.

In short, Anna is an outstanding young woman. She has shown great ability in academic learning. She will surely be the pillar of the state, if she is granted enrollment in your university for further study. Therefore, I strongly recommend her and appreciate your assistance with her application.

Sincerely,

Prof. David White

Department of ….

Address:

5

To whom it may concern:

It is a great pleasure for me to recommend Mr. Ted Morris to your graduate program. He is a senior undergraduate student of the Biology Department, at the University of Georgia, and I have come to know him better since he passed a xxx Course with me last semester.

Ted's strong academic record, especially in his field of study, is a true indication of his seriousness and intention to pursue his studies. He participated in xxx course and expressed great interest and ability in acquiring knowledge and performing research during this course. This potential talent and enthusiasm resulted in an outstanding research on "xxx" at the end of the semester, which was a comprehensive report gathered through studying various related papers and articles.

In my experience with Ted, I have found him quite competent, hardworking, and independent, with an eagerness to reach the highest degrees in his favorite fields. One should be of superior capability and exceptional talent to get the 1st rank in xxx field at University of xxx.

Considering all the above facts, I strongly recommend Ted for admission to your graduate program. His outstanding background and his research abilities and interest in gaining knowledge in his field of study guarantee his prosperity, and I am confident that your program will benefit from having him as a graduate student.

Sincerely,

Luke Ray

University of Georgia

Address:

January 9, 2011

6

January 5, 2010

Admissions, Wax School of Management

Executive MBA Program

123 City Center, St. A44

Houston, TX   75242-7700

To whom it may concern:

I am impressed with Mary More's enthusiasm, communication skills, and professional demeanor. She entered our graduate program two years ago and during this program, she has consistently kept her GPA at the highest level. This demonstrates her academic qualities and capabilities. Therefore, I heartily endorse her for any PhD position in Business and Management and related areas.

Mary participated in my xxx class last semester. She has also finished her master thesis on xxx under my supervision. She has demonstrated remarkable academic and research abilities in her project. She is dependable, trustworthy, and obedient.

It is for these reasons that I offer high recommendations for Mary without reservation. If you have any questions regarding this recommendation, please do not hesitate to contact me.

Sincerely,

Claire Ruiz

Associate Professor at University of Houston

7

February 4, 2010

To whom it may concern:

I am pleased to recommend Betty Taylor, who has been a student in my MIS and Research Methods classes for the past two semesters. Betty is an exceptional student who can work in a research team or independently. She is reliable, dedicated, and eternally upbeat.

Organized and diligent, Betty quickly learns new things. She often exhibited excellent leadership in my class, volunteering to lead groups and then organizing the group's project quickly and efficiently. In addition, Betty multitasks effectively and is able to successfully handle a high-volume workload.

In short, Betty has earned a reputation as a hardworking, trustworthy individual who strives to excel. She responds with courage when challenged to produce her best. I regret that I only had the pleasure of coaching her a single year.

As you can tell, I am impressed with this outstanding young lady. Therefore, I give her my strongest recommendation for roles that require intelligence, communication skills, and a positive attitude.

Sincerely,

Stephen B. Garrett

Professor of Management at …

8

To whom it may concern:

This letter is to serve as my formal recommendation for Joseph Riche. He has been my teaching assistant for the last two years. He is interested in continuing his studies toward a PhD degree. I believe he would be an excellent candidate for your esteemed program.

During his time here in our department, Joseph has consistently demonstrated strong research capabilities and a dedication to success. His efforts have produced high quality results time and time again. His brilliant ideas have helped us to improve the quality of our graduate degrees and to gain our students' satisfaction.

Though Joseph is working as a teaching assistant, his social and leadership abilities encourage his co-workers and students to seek his advice and support and Joseph is always there for them. I am confident that the combination of his strong academic background and his budding leadership abilities make him an exceptional candidate for PhD studies.

For these reasons, I strongly encourage you to give Joseph Riche's application a favorable review. If there is any question, or if I can be of any other assistance, please contact me at your earliest convenience.

Sincerely,

Sophia Jones

Department of ….. at …..

Email:

Tel:

9

Aaron Harris
123 AB Street
City center, TX 12345

September 11, 2012

To whom it may concern:

As the graduate adviser of Yale University, I have had the pleasure of knowing Kati Raff for the last two years when she became a graduate student in our department. During this course, she has been a tremendous student. Therefore, I would like to take this opportunity to recommend her for your PhD program in IT Management.

Kati's determination to succeed has led her to excel in my classes. She consistently received excellent marks on her homework and tests, and she participates regularly in class. Her knowledge of basic theories of Information Technology convinced me to ask her to become a tutor for other students who were struggling with the course—a challenge that she met with great success. The students she tutored significantly improved their grades, and some have even chosen IT as their majors.

Compared to the other students in class, Kati's grades have always been at the top. This has led other students in her classes to ask her for help if they do not understand a lesson. Despite her busy schedule, Kati always balances her time so she can help anyone who needs assistance with the lessons.

I feel confident Kati will continue to succeed in her studies. She is not only a dedicated, hardworking, and intelligent student, but she is also personally delightful. She is equally comfortable with her peers and with the faculty.

It is for these reasons that I offer high recommendations for Kati Raff without reservation. Her academic abilities will truly be an asset to your program. I am happy to provide further information if required.

Sincerely,

Emma Hall

Professor of IT Management at ... University

June 18, 2009

Admissions, Max School of Mathematics

100 Pomeraz Center, Ste E44

XX City, TX   12345-7700

Dear Professor Baker,

This reference letter is provided at the written request of Eric Koja, who has asked me to serve as a reference on his behalf. It is my understanding that Eric is being considered by your department for graduate study in Mathematics.

I have known Eric for the past two years as he has taken the following courses, which I teach: Statistics I, Statistics II, and General Mathematics. As his professor, I have had an opportunity to observe his participation and interaction in class. I would rate his overall performance in these subjects as outstanding. This is evidenced by his high GPA grades (3.8).

I know first-hand that Eric performs with aplomb in challenging situations. His brilliant communication skills and his strong academic capabilities make him an exceptional candidate for graduate studies. In short, Eric's high caliber of character and keen meteorological expertise set him well above others at his level of education. Therefore, I warmly recommend Eric for your graduate program. If you would like to discuss this further, please feel free to contact me.

Sincerely,

Professor William Collins, Ph.D.

Email: XXX

Tel: 000-000-0000

11

To whom it may concern:

I am writing in enthusiastic support of Steven Iler. I have been teaching at the University of xxx for the last three years. During this time, Steven has been among the talented and hardworking students. He was an exceptional student and extremely quick in grasping the concepts and ideas. He is keen to learn new things. He is a hardworking person, works well with people, and is courteous and dependable.

Steven has finished his final project on xxx under my direct supervision, and received a high grade. As his supervisor, I have seen his endeavors and efforts to conduct a high valued research. He accomplishes his tasks with great initiative and with a positive attitude. He is also organized and reliable.

Without any doubt, Steven would make an excellent addition to your program. I recommend him without hesitation. Should you have any questions, please feel free to contact me.

Sincerely,

Eli Smith

November 3, 2010

12

Jack King

5001 B Johnson Fwy
Miami, FL 12345
(214) 123-1234

January 15, 2010

Dear Professor Bella Lewis,

It is with great pleasure that I am writing this letter in support of Mr. Kevin Haner's application to participate in your research program in Operation Research. Kevin is a student in Management Science at xxx University. Currently, he is pursuing a Master Degree in our department and it is expected to finish it next semester. Kevin possesses a perfect 4.0 GPA. He has shown significant aptitude in performing research in our university. He is working on xxx for his master thesis under my supervision. During this course, I have seen that he is growing both academically and personally.

Kevin possesses a positive and enthusiastic personality. He has great empathy with his classmates and the faculty. He is confident, knowledgeable, and has the skills of a seasoned researcher. He is well equipped to grow from the challenges he is presented with. I am confident his strong academic background and brilliant ideas will make him an exceptional student.

Given the above facts, I wholeheartedly recommend this talented man to your program. Please contact me if there is anything else I can do on his behalf.

Sincerely,

Prof. Jack King, Ph.D.

13

December 24, 2011

To whom it may concern:

It is a great pleasure for me to write this reference letter for Mr. James Rutledge to attend your university for the graduate program. I have known him since 2006, Second Semester as an undergraduate student in our department. He has taken xxx course with me, obtaining an outstanding result (3.9) as a result of his brilliant performance in the exams and in the assignments. This becomes more significant when you may notice that he ranked first in his class of about 50 students. He also accomplished his final course project about xxx, with feedback, successfully.

It is worth mentioning that James has always been among our top students in the department during his undergraduate and graduate studies. His high GPA is a good indicator of his strong academic background. In addition, he is intelligent, hardworking, and disciplined with a pleasant personality.

Given the above facts, I believe that James has potential to make a good accomplishment and contributions to your program. I, therefore, unreservedly recommend Mr. James Rutledge to you for any kind of assistantship or scholarship.

Sincerely Yours,

Professor Ashely Reed

14

To whom it may concern

I am proud to recommend a beloved student, Robert Thomas, for your Ph.D. program in Marketing. I have known him for three years in my capacity as Professor, Department of Computer Science. I have also taught him several courses including "xxx", "xxx", and "xxx", and I am his direct supervisor for his master thesis.

During his studies, I worked closely with Robert. As a result, I have become very familiar with him. Accordingly, I am writing this because it is my earnest belief that he is eminently qualified for your program.

Robert is a talented and hardworking student. His records as a Teaching Assistant (TA) and his willingness for further studies show his qualifications for original work and research. His interests include xxx, xxx, and related areas in which he is strongly recommended as a graduate applicant.

In closing, I recommend Robert for further studies in your graduate program. I can assure you of his competence for original work and research in his proposed field of study. If you would like further elaboration, feel free to call me at xxx.

Sincerely,

Sarah Perez

Professor of xxx

15

March 1, 2011

To whom it may concern:

It is a distinct pleasure to recommend Edward Morgan for graduate work in the fields of Management and Business. Ranked first in the entrance exam to graduate studies in Business Administration, he is expected to complete all the requirements for the degree of Master of Science by June 2011.

In my capacity as an associate professor at xxx Business School, I have worked closely with Edward for more than two years. During this time, I have found him to be a multi-faceted person. He is distinguished for a number of important achievements during his course of study in our department. For one thing, he has ranked first among his entering class of 2009 with an outstanding GPA (3.92).

Edward has also been successful in social relationships. His sense of organization can be helpful in a team project. He is able to successfully complete multiple tasks with favorable results despite deadline pressure.

Considering all the facts, I recommend Mr. Edward Morgan for your graduate school with absolutely no reservations. I believe he will be eminently successful in his future academic endeavors.

Sincerely,

Levi Cox, Ph.D.

Department of xxx at xxx

16

Bill Jackson

123 Main St

Los Angeles

(123) 456-7891

August 4, 2006

To whom it may concern:

This letter of recommendation has been written in support of Mr. Kaya Thomas' application to your graduate school of engineering. I have known him since February 2009, when he started to work on his M.S. thesis under my direct supervision. His thesis subject was "xxx". Kaya conducted his thesis successfully with a high grade (3.8).

During this time, I have found Kaya to be an enthusiastic researcher, and keen to elaborate conceptual ideas. His wide understanding of electronics concepts and work experience make him a successful Ph.D. candidate. In addition, he possesses the capacity to contribute positively, while working as part of a team.

It is clear to me that this young researcher, Kaya Tomas, is an exceptional candidate, one that would contribute greatly to your

Ph.D. program. He deserves to be awarded any kind of research or teaching assistantship.

Sincerely,

Prof. Bill Jackson, Department of xxx

17

TO WHOM IT MAY CONCERN:

It is my sincere pleasure to recommend Bernard Miller for a master's program in Industrial Engineering at your University. I have known him as a senior member of our research team since February 2008. During this period, Bernard has been involved in Accomplishment of Energy Subsidy Project under my supervision at the xxx research center. Bernard has performed a brilliant contribution within our team. In addition to his excellent academic capabilities, he has shown strong leadership and social capabilities.

Bernard has impressed me as being an intelligent and creative researcher with a pleasant personality. He is very easy to work with, enthusiastically participates in discussions, and develops novel ideas. He has shown to be quite innovative in finding solutions for challenging problems we faced. I would like to recommend him for graduate studies in your university, especially in the field of xxx. Please do not hesitate to contact me for further information.

Sincerely,

Payton James

18

January 30, 2011

To whom it may concern:

I would like to recommend Miss Jane Lampard for your graduate program in Operation Research. A bright student, Jane started her college education in September 2008, after she placed second in the entrance exam. So far, Jane has passed 188 hours of course work and has compiled a GPA of 3.72. As an undergraduate student, Jane has taken two courses with me and has earned very good grades, 3.75 and 3.8.

Jane has also taken as a teaching assistant for two semesters with a colleague of mine. During this time, she has demonstrated notable academic and social skills. I believe that her strong academic background makes her an exceptional candidate for graduate studies.

Since September 2009, Jane has joined a team that is responsible for evaluating the national energy subsidy program. In this team, she has shown an excellent performance and I am seeing her rapid progress.

On the personal side, I have known Jane to be a mature student who is well liked by her teachers and classmates. She is capable of working with others on group projects. Based on Jane Lampard's qualifications, I would recommend her to place on your graduate program and I think that she will be quite successful as a graduate student as well.

Sincerely,

Arianna Powell

Associate Professor at xxx

19

Subject: Recommendation Letter for Mr. John Smith

Date: 01/09/2011

To whom it may concern:

This letter is intended to serve as a recommendation for Mr. John Smith. My acquaintance with John started in the fall of 2008. He was my student in the "Organizational Design" course. In my class, he caught my attention by participating in all the sessions and by showing great interest in taking part in class discussions. In addition, this course had a demanding project that counted for 50% of the total grade. This project has always been of great help to me in evaluating my students objectively. I grade these projects on their technical merits and on the student's ability to convince the reader of the validity of the project. John earned a very good grade in the class on this project (3.8). In September of 2009, I chose him as one of my teaching assistants in MIS course.

John has my highest recommendations. He possesses a pleasant personality. He is sincere, thorough, and reliable in meeting objectives and deadlines. Based on my acquaintance with him, I am confident John will be successful in his future academic endeavors in the field of industrial engineering or related subject.

It is my hope that you will accept his admission to your university.

Feel free to contact me if you require further information.

Sincerely yours,

Stella Foster

Associate Professor at xxx

Address:

Email:

20

To whom it may concern:

This is in response to your recent request for a letter of recommendation for Nina Holt. She has taken two courses with me here at the University of xxx, as an undergraduate student. She has received good grades in both of them (3.7 and 3.76).

Nina has also been my assistant in MIS (Management Information Systems) course for two semesters. During this period, she has convinced me of her capability in performing her assignment through her in-depth understanding of the objectives. I have found her a hardworking, bright, energetic, and sociable student.

If your undergraduate program is seeking superior candidates with a record of achievement, Nina is an excellent choice. Based on her enthusiasm, I would like to recommend her for your M.S. program in Management. I believe that she can be a successful student.

Sincerely yours,

Aaron Ellis

Professor of Management at xxx

21

To whom it may concern:

This letter is intended to serve as a recommendation for Mr. Ted Beck. My acquaintance with Ted started in the fall of 2009. He was my student in the "HRM" course, and has been my teaching assistant since June of 2010.

Ted showed his great interest in graduate studies by participating in all of my classes and by taking part in class discussions. In addition, he earned the highest grade in the class. Because I grade the students on their written and verbal communication skills, I can assert that Ted has a brilliant social and communication capability. Therefore, I chose him as my teaching assistant in a several courses such as HRM and Organizational Behavior. Although it was his first experience, he learned academic skills very quickly. I also found Ted to be a reliable team leader.

After two years of working with Ted, I have no doubt that his diligence, talent, and enthusiasm will lead him to learn much more in his chosen field of study. Based on his analysis capacities, I am confident he is able to become a successful academic professional in the field of Management and Business.

In closing, as detailed above, based on my experience working with him, I can unreservedly recommend Ted Beck to you for your graduate program. If you have any questions, please feel free to contact me.

Sincerely yours,

Maya Ford, Professor of Business

Accounting and Management Department

22

March 1, 2009

Dear Professor Brianna Webb

It is my pleasure to recommend Mr. John Nevil for admission to your PhD program in Business Administration. I came to know John when he was my student in an IT course two years ago. John distinguished himself by submitting an exceptionally well researched and interesting project on an eCommerce topic. Therefore, I ranked him in the top 2% of students I have taught in the past three years, particularly concerning his research skills.

Overall, John is highly intelligent and has excellent analytical skills. His project demonstrated his ability to come to a thorough understanding of IT and its increasingly important role in business. He gave a particularly interesting discussion of the difficult practice of eCommerce. His overall intelligence is also reflected in his grades for the course, which were by far the best in the class.

John has excellent social skills. His clear, concise, and interesting presentations grab all audiences' attention. He is also a good writer. His writings are well structured and easy to follow. He always explains his views very concisely and gives supporting arguments that are clear and persuasive. John also demonstrated noble team working skills in group assignments.

On a personal level, John is a disciplined student with a pleasant personality. He goes well beyond the course requirements in the quantity and quality of his project, putting in a lot of extra research and attending office hours every week. Throughout the course, John showed perseverance and initiative. He was not only interested in and motivated to learn the material, but also put great work into assimilating it to his own experience and developing his own ideas about each topic we discussed. John is unquestionably an exceptional candidate for graduate study in Business and Management. His work in HRM and MIS courses suggests that he would benefit from the opportunities provided in your graduate program. He has proven himself to have the perseverance and initiative, and the intellectual creativity necessary to complete an advanced graduate degree.

I would therefore highly recommend John Nevil. I am confident that his performance in my class is a good indication of how he would perform as a graduate student. If I can be of any further assistance, or provide you with any further information, please do not hesitate to contact me.

Yours sincerely,

Jose Mason

23

Dear Prof. John Smith

Department of Accounting and Management

It gives me immense pleasure in recommending Mr. Ken Hale for the graduate program in Computer Science at your university. I have known him for four years in my capacity as a professor in the department of Computer and IT Studies. I have also taught him two theory courses, "Introduction to Information Technology" and "Management Information Systems".

Based on his performance records, he can be placed in the top 10% of students in the class. He is smart, inquisitive, and desires to gain an in-depth knowledge. With his talent and hard work, I have no doubt that he will succeed in all his endeavors.

His project on Computer Networks Security conducted at our university was ranked among the best projects carried out in the department at master level. He has shown the inspiration, intelligence, and analytical aptitude for graduate studies and research. He owns the capacity to contribute positively, while working as part of a team.

Ken compares favorably with the best among my students. I am sure he will make an outstanding graduate student. Therefore, I recommend him in the strongest terms for admission to your graduate program.

Sincerely,

Prof. Faith Holmes

Department of xxx

24

January 23, 2010

To whom it may concern:

It is with enthusiasm and enjoyment that I am writing to support Nora Holt's application to the USD master program in ecology. For over 30 years, I have supervised many research laboratories and counseled many students seeking professional advancement. I hope my view of Nora will be beneficial to the USD admissions committee as you evaluate this exceptional candidate.

I first encountered Nora during the spring semester of 2009, when she entered my office needing advice over respective class scheduling. During our discussion, she presented the idea that she would like to continue her studies in ecology. It was apparent at the time that she was motivated to achieve her academic goals.

During the time I have known Nora, she has shown energetic enthusiasm for learning and an openness to new ideas. She was a student in different courses of my class schedule. In these classes, she demonstrated an eagerness for academic endeavors. She scored at the top of her class on all verbal and written examinations during this time.

Since then, I have asked Nora to work as my teaching assistant. She proved herself a leader among her peers and was responsible for assisting students, examining and grading. Her skills were apparent to all.

I know Nora is highly motivated and interested in her research areas. She has fulfilled the degree requirements of our university with exceptional scores and enhanced the ecology sciences program. I have the highest admiration for her achievements. I advise you to thoughtfully consider her application.

Sincerely,

Jace Mills, Ph.D.

Professor of Ecology

25

To whom it may concern:

I have had the distinct pleasure of having Micheal Jons as an accounting assistant from December 2008 to September 2010. His responsibilities include setting up new clients for review, writing brief summaries of their financial condition, and managing the secretarial staff. During his employment, Micheal exemplified a hard worker and a talented asset to the staff.

Micheal's efficiency, time management, and social skills have impressed me. His quick understanding of the various tasks presented was comprehensive. Moreover, his concise and thought provoking writing skills allowed insightful views of clients and clear financial outlines.

Your program of study sounds ideally suited to Micheal's academic goals. He will be coming to you with the proven groundwork necessary for success in pursuing an MBA. He will also bring his interest in accounting and marketing. It is exciting to think of the many ways Micheal will be able to contribute to other students and the faculty.

I highly recommend Micheal Jons for your program and hope that you will carefully consider his admission application.

Sincerely,

Peter Williams

Chief Accountant for xxx

December 3, 2010

To whom it may concern:

This letter is to serve as my formal recommendation for Mr. Tom Richardson. My acquaintance with Tom started in 2008. He was my student in the "Fuzzy Logic" course, and my research assistant in the spring 2009.

In my class, Tom participated in all the sessions and was very active in taking part in class discussions. He finally scored A^+ in this class. During the course, Tom demonstrated his great interest in fuzzy clustering. He developed his ideas under my supervision and submitted a paper on this issue to a prestigious journal.

I have no doubt that Tom's diligence, talent, and enthusiasm will lead him to learn much more in his chosen field of study. Based on my acquaintance with him, I am confident he is able to become a capable researcher and will have a successful academic fortune. I would like to whole-heartedly and strongly recommend him to your graduate program and hope that you will carefully consider his application.

Sincerely Yours,

Prof. Ahmed Abed

Department of Computer Science

To whom it may concern:

I have known Jacob Miles as a senior member of our research team in the Biomechanics Lab, during the years 2007-2010. During this time, Jacob was systematically involved in a variety of research activities under my supervision. These researches have been mainly in the field of design and implementation of image-processing techniques.

Jacob performed a bright contribution within this team as a system analyst with high programming skills and technical knowledge. He also conducted a comprehensive technology review and evaluated the different techniques for xxx, in an industry-internship project performed under my supervision in collaboration with xxx Company.

Along with his significant research activities, Jacob has a proud academic history. In 2006, he was ranked second in the National Informatics entrance exam. He was also among top 1% students in his class.

Jacob has impressed me as being an exceptionally intelligent and creative researcher with pleasant personality. He is very easy to work with, enthusiastically participates in discussions, and develops novel ideas. I would like to recommend him for graduate studies, especially in the field of xxx.

Sincerely,

Andrea Dunn

Address:

Email:

Mobile:

28

To whom it may concern:

I met Mr. Michael Park in Fall 2007 when he participated in my course of xxx. He subsequently undertook his master thesis under my direct supervision, entitled "xxx". I am pleased to confirm that Michael is an outstanding student at University of xxx, which is known as the best engineering school in the country. From the start, he grasped the fundamentals quickly and moved on to develop new original techniques. He has shown to be quite innovative in finding solutions to new problems he faces. Because of his talent and hard work, he submitted several journal papers in his research area. Moreover, he has several published and submitted conference papers in some international and local conferences.

In addition to his excellent academic capacities, Michael has also shown strong social capabilities. He has efficiently participated in social activities at the organization of xxx.

It is worth mentioning that Michael finished high school in a well-known school in 2006, and ranked fourth in the university of xxx's undergraduate entrance exam among the 2,000 participants. He is a very challenging, and conscientious student and I really enjoyed having him in my research group. I believe that he has a strong theoretical background and excellent enthusiasm, punctuality, and intelligibility to pursue his studies towards a Ph.D. degree. Therefore, I sincerely recommend him as the ideal candidate for your program in xxx.

Respectfully submitted,

Alex Payne

To whom it may concern:

Ms. Sara Smith is applying for admission to your Ph.D. program in Electrical Engineering. I am writing this letter to support her application. She entered our master program in 2008 and currently completing her thesis under my direct supervision. I also had her in two graduate courses (xxx and xxx). Sara was excellent in my courses and I found her very intelligent, serious, orderly, hardworking, and independent. She is competent, motivated, and responsible and she works hard to reach her goals.

Sara is very interested in Ph.D. studies. Given her talents and interests, I believe that she will have a successful graduate education once she is given the chance. Considering all the facts, I would like to strongly recommend her for your consideration of offering her admission to your graduate program.

Sincerely,

Luis Stone, Professor of xxx

Department of xxx

January 3, 2010

May 9, 2011

To whom it may concern:

It is a great pleasure for me to write this reference for Peter Garland. I met Peter Summer 2009 when he undertook his B.S. project under my supervision in the field of xxx entitled as: "xxx".

I am pleased to confirm that Peter is an outstanding student in our university, which is known as one the best engineering schools and admits the best high school and graduate students. During this time, Peter has shown to be quite innovative. As a result, he developed brilliant ideas in his research study in the field of xxx. He has also published several journal papers in the best journals in this field of research.

In addition to his excellent academic abilities, Peter has shown strong leadership and social capabilities. He efficiently participated in organizing a workshop on "xxx", held at xxx University in Summer 2010.

Peter is a conscientious student. I believe he has a strong theoretical background and excellent enthusiasm to pursue his studies.

I rank him in the range of the top 2% of my students and I strongly recommend him for the applied postgraduate studies. I am confident that he will be able to satisfy a high educational standard at the graduate level as well.

I would be happy to provide additional details or comments that might be required.

Yours sincerely,

Prof. Nolan Rose, Ph.D.

31

To whom it may concern:

It is my great pleasure to recommend Gary Joe for graduate studies in the field of Material Science at your university. I have known him for the past four years. I had the chance to supervise his B.Sc. project titled "xxx". He received a score of 3.8 on his project. During this time, I realized that he is clever and independent in research activities. Gary has also a strong background for doing research and he is very hardworking.

Working as a consultant in a well-known company such as UTQ is an indication that Gary will be an excellent researcher in his field of study. He is also an effective team player and goes out of his way to help his colleagues.

Based on his academic background, I highly recommend Gary for a PhD program in the field of Material Science.

Sincerely yours,

Molly Rice

Associate Professor, xxx University

32

September 4, 2008

To whom it may concern:

I would like to recommend Lisa Potter as a PhD candidate to your program in Computer Science. I have known this young lady since June, 2008. She was my student in xxx course. Lisa was an active and conscientious member of the class. She challenged the rest of the class to consider issues from new perspectives and often asked very penetrating and important questions. She chose to take on difficult topics and handled them well. Her assignments were well written, well-supported, organized, neat, and timely. It was evident that she really desired to learn more and challenge herself.

Lisa also has interests outside of academics. She has been an active member of the Student Association in our university. She is also a member of the xxx society. Her personality is wonderful. She is outgoing and friendly, but not dominating. She has an obvious and sincere concern for others.

I feel very confident that Lisa will be successful in all her future endeavors. She is a focused and determined young woman. Therefore, I highly recommend her for your graduate program.

Sincerely,

Piper Reyes

33

January 3, 2010

To whom it may concern:

I am pleased to write to you on behalf of Susan Moore, who is applying for a fellowship to study Mathematics. I have known her for two years. She took my course in xxx. More recently, I have been advising her on her thesis.

Susan has done well in both her courses' assignments and her thesis. She has had substantial exposure to the practical aspects of her topic. I have witnessed that she was extremely well prepared to fulfill her proposed project. Susan has selected an area that is of growing interest. In my point of view, her research topic seems to be both worthwhile and feasible.

Susan is an independent self-starter. Although she has no trouble working in groups, or interacting with others, she can also work well on her own. She is a very congenial person, well-liked by teachers and students in our department, and you will see why I am so positive about this lovely and energetic young lady.

I endorse her candidacy with confidence and enthusiasm. I hope that you will consider her application strongly.

Sincerely,

Sydney Dixon

To whom it may concern:

This letter is in support of Donna Martin, who is applying for a PhD position in MIS. She has recently finished her thesis under my direct supervision. I have had many discussions with her about her research, which I find both compelling and important. Her research's focus of interest, the role of new technologies in sustainable development, is admirably suited to someone of Donna's talents and intelligence.

During the last 15 months, I have found Donna to be a very intelligent and hardworking student. She is capable of cooperating in a research team. Personally, she is polite and pleasant person to work with. I would expect her to perform well in a wide range of environments. In fact, her academic history should place her high on any list of PhD candidates in MIS and related areas.

Given the above facts, I believe Donna will make significant accomplishments and contributions in your program and her graduate studies. She deserves to be awarded any kind of scholarship or fellowship.

Sincerely,

Jack Burns, Ph.D.

To whom it may concern:

I am delighted to recommend Mr. William Hanks, a highly intelligent and studious young man, for admission to your university program. In my capacity as his advisor, I have worked closely with him for two years and witnessed his quick development and growth.

William is devoted, skilled, creative, joyful and a pleasure to work with. I appreciate and support his desire to continue his education as a PhD student in a well-equipped university.

William has some personality traits distinguishing him from other students. He is a charismatic leader whose objective is to serve other people. He always strives to resolve student's difficulties, and think of them as a part of his life. He is also a good motivator, and uses his best endeavors to promote student efficiency.

William is very interested in continuing his research at a higher level and he has spared no effort to achieve this goal. If your graduate program is seeking the best candidates, without a doubt, William is a suitable choice. He has persistently exhibited and proved his merit to succeed in many tasks and projects.

I sincerely recommend that you consider his application carefully. I am confident William will make an outstanding PhD student. If you have any question regarding this recommendation, please do not hesitate to contact me.

Sincerely,

Professor Kayla Boyd

Address:

Email: xxx

Mobile: xxx

John Sutton

123 Serra

Mall Stanford, CA 94305

(123) 456-1234

December 08, 2011

To whom it may concern:

I would like to take this opportunity to write this recommendation in support of Betsy Lucas' application for your graduate program. I have known this talented and motivated student since she entered our undergraduate program in Information Technology. She took the course titled "Study of IS and IT Management" with me. She received excellent grade in this course as a result of her outstanding performance. She was always participating in the class discussions providing her challenging questions and brilliant ideas.

I have found Betsy as an intelligent student capable of cooperating in a research team. She is a student who can conduct her research with a minimal guidance and is capable of facing new challenges.

She is organized and with high motivation for graduate studies. In addition, she is very polite and well disciplined.

Given the above facts, I believe Betsy will make very good accomplishments and contributions to your program. I, therefore, strongly recommend her and recommend you consider her application carefully.

Sincerely yours,

Assistance Prof. John Sutton

To whom it may concern:

It is a great pleasure for me to recommend Mr. Amir Behbahani for a graduate program in Electrical Engineering at your university. I have known him since he participated in my xxx course. During this short time, I have found Amir an intelligent, serious, orderly, and hardworking student. He is competent, motivated, and responsible, and he works hard to reach his goals. He is interested in applied research activities.

Amir is a polite person with pleasant personality. He interacts well with the other students and the staff of the university. He also has good communication skills, both verbally and orally. I found him as a good presenter and speaker.

Given his talents and interests, I believe he will have a successful graduate education once he is given the chance. Considering all the facts, I would like to strongly recommend him in your consideration of offering his admission to your graduate program.

Sincerely,

Ian Henry, Professor of xxx

38

To whom it may concern:

I am pleased to recommend Mitt Paterson for postgraduate studies in the field of Materials Science and Engineering. I have known Mitt for more than three years while he was participating in my advanced phase transformation course and during his education in our M.Sc. program. During this period, he has shown himself as a hardworking, enthusiastic, and talented student with brilliant academic background. I found him to be a cooperative person and capable of working with others on team research projects.

Based on my knowledge of Mitt's academic background in our school, I would like to strongly recommend him for post-graduate studies at your institute. I would appreciate it if you give a favorable response to his application.

Sincerely yours,

Chase Hicks, Professor of xxx

School of xxx

March 11, 2011

39

Subject: Letter of Reference

To whom it may concern:

This is a letter of reference prepared to support Mr. Harry Kings, who has been my student from early 2008 to date. Since his arrival in my lab, Harry has become involved in a work on xxx using standard xxx solutions. This work was our first experience on this subject and Harry showed his exceptional talent in bringing this rather established subject into a challenging and hectic matter.

Harry has also been my student in the course of Electronic, where his mark was excellent. I am aware that his overall average is not the best (around 3.1). This rather poor performance in his courses is not something compatible with the talents I have seen in his research work. I am sure that he can rectify himself to achieve higher performance in his future courses and show that a person with that level of understanding can handle standard course materials, without serious difficulty.

I have found Harry to be a sincere, hardworking, and industrious person with the ability to engage in teamwork without any difficulty. He takes advice whenever needed and acts accordingly. He is certainly one of the best researchers and I am proud of his performance as an undergraduate student. He is fond of research and dedicates himself to its adventure.

In closing, Harry Kings is a tenacious, talented, hardworking, and superior person with plenty of potentials and strengths. I do recommend him for your graduate program without reservation.

Best regards,

Lauren Simpson, Associate Professor,

Department of Electrical and Computer Engineering

May 04, 2010

40

To whom it may concern:

This letter of recommendation has been written in support of Paul Kinz's application for admission to your Master's Program. I have known him since he was a B.S. student in our department. He has taken a couple of courses with me. In these courses, I have found him to be a talented and motivated student.

Paul is an enthusiastic researcher in the field of Computer Sciences. In addition, he has a great ability in developing Information systems and Analyzing Systems. He is successful in teamwork and independent work and has been an active member in organizing and developing software projects in our faculty. Therefore, I strongly recommend him for your MS program without any reservation.

Sincerely,

Julia Tucker

Assistant Professor, Dept. of xxx

Phone: xxx

Email: xxx

41

January 14, 2010

To whom it may concern,

I would like to take an opportunity to offer a formal recommendation for Mr. Tom Christenson, the applicant to your graduate studies program. I have known Tom since he was my student in Circuits Theory course in 2009. Tom demonstrated a brilliant performance in this course and received the best score (4).

He also took the xxx course with me and got the same score. His intelligence and dedication makes him capable of gaining precious experiences within his studies in our department. Tom has been a teaching assistant in several courses and has shown a remarkable performance. His achievement in keeping his GPA uniformly high during his studies is an important aspect of his academic capabilities.

He is now a research assistant in xxx Lab, where he is involved in different projects about vertical transistors. Based on his personal and educational background, I have no reservation to recommend him for any graduate education in Electrical Engineering and related areas.

Sincerely,

Colton Murray, Ph.D.

Professor of xxx

42

To whom it may concern:

This is a letter of reference in support of Mr. Mark Lee, the applicant to your graduate studies program. I have known Mark for about three years, from the time he was my student in xxx and xxx, with outstanding performance.

He also took the xxx course with me in which he gained the first rank in his class. His intelligence and dedication makes him capable of gaining precious experiences in his field of studies.

I also would like to mention his originality in the work and his analytical ability and clearance in judgment. For these reasons, I have no reservation to recommend him for any graduate education in Electrical Engineering and related areas.

Sincerely,

Ayden Gomes

Professor of xxx

43

Stella Hunter

123 College Eight Road

Santa Cruz, CA 95064

June 24, 2012

To whom it may concern:

I am proud to recommend a beloved student, Josef Richardson, for your graduate program. I have known Josef for more than two years. He has been my student in the "xxx" course, in which his results were outstanding; he obtained 3.9. He was always actively participating in discussions throughout the course. He took "xxx" course with me and he has scored impressive grade of 4. In fact, his performance during these courses was exceptional. He also had an excellent final project about xxx. In his project, Josef demonstrated his brilliant ideas.

He has been my TA in several courses with the main responsibility for handling and assessing assignments and quizzes, and helping students with their projects. He was able to manage all his tasks with remarkable efforts.

I have found Josef to be an active student in university life as well. He is a member of xxx association from 2007 and he was an active organizer in third International Conference on xxx. Personally, he is a well-organized, intelligent, and hardworking person.

Regarding the above, I have no reservation to recommend Josef for any graduate studies in Electrical Engineering. Please feel free to contact me via email if you need further information.

Sincerely,

Stella Hunter

Associate Professor, Department of xxx

Email:

Phone:

44

To whom it may concern:

It gives me immense pleasure in recommending Gary Milner for the admission to your Ph.D. program in Management Science. As the professor of Management at xxx University, I work closely with many of the graduate students. I consider Gary to be one of the most studious and responsible students of our department. He has done two projects on xxx and xxx in a group of four members under my supervision. Because of their efforts, they have received an A grade and Gary played an important role to gain this result.

I have found Gary as an intelligent student capable of cooperating in a research team. He is a student who can conduct his research with a minimal guidance, capable of facing new challenges, and finding good solutions for difficult problems. He is organized and with high motivation for graduate studies. In addition, he is polite and disciplined with an enjoyable personality.

Given the above facts, I believe Gary will make a good contribution to your research programs. Therefore, I strongly recommend him for your graduate program. He deserves to be awarded any kind of assistantship, scholarship, or fellowship.

Sincerely yours,

Scarlett Ortiz

Address:

Email:

August 15, 2010

45

December 03, 2010

To whom it may concern:

It is my pleasure to write this letter of recommendation for Mr. Adnan Sharif, who is an applicant to your graduate studies program. Adnan has worked toward completing a research project on xxx under my supervision for about a year. During this research interaction with him, I have found Adnan to be a highly enthusiastic student capable of doing research and pursuing graduate studies. During his undergraduate studies, Adnan was among the top 5% of his class, illustrating his academic capabilities. He has also obtained the third rank in his class, which is a good indication of his high potential.

In his work under my supervision on xxx, he did a comprehensive study on the xxx methods. He has conceived a new method for xxx. He also had a chance to submit his work to a prestigious international conference in 2009.

Given the above facts, I believe that Adnan will make great contributions to your research groups and his graduate studies.

Therefore, I strongly recommend him for your graduate program, preferably with financial aid.

Sincerely yours,

Charles Cruz

Electrical and Computer department

University of xxx

Address:

Email:

Phone:

46

Subject: Recommendation Letter

Jaxon Gibson

P.O. Box 12345.

Fullerton, **CA** 92834-9480.

December 09, 2011

To whom it may concern:

I am very pleased to recommend Mr. Ahmad Jamal for admission to your Ph.D. program in Industrial Engineering. I have known him since he was a B.S. student in our department and I served as his academic advisor. He was also my assistant in "xxx" course. During his M.Sc. study, he took my graduate course in "xxx" and obtained 3.75, the first grade among 65 students as a result of a good performance in the exams and in the course project.

Although he is an enthusiastic researcher in the field of xxx, he has taken several courses in xxx, xxx, and xxx providing him with a strong background in all areas of Electronics. In addition, he has a great ability in problem analysis, making him quite capable of facing new challenges.

Ahmad is successful in teamwork and independent work and has been an active member in organizing conferences, seminars, and workshops in our department. He is also an intelligent and hardworking person in research, while soft in social activities. Ahmad is a trustworthy individual and would be an excellent candidate for your school.

Sincerely,

Professor Jaxon Gibson

Dept. of xxx

Phone:

47

To whom it may concern:

It gives me great satisfaction to recommend Mr. Paul Kroger for admission to your Ph.D. program. I was Paul's professor in three undergraduate Communications courses and worked closely with him for the last three years. He has obtained the perfect grade in all courses as a result of his good performance in the exams and in the course project. He was also very active in the class sessions of the course.

He has done two projects on "xxx" in a group of three members. Because of their noble efforts, they have managed to provide a remarkable project results and submit several journal and conference papers. Paul is doing his M.S. thesis on "xxx" under my direct supervision and I see his rapid growth in research and academic in the field of xxx.

Although he is an enthusiastic researcher in the field of xxx, Paul's strong background in all areas of xxx makes him an appropriate PhD candidate. I have found Paul to be an intelligent and hardworking student, capable of cooperating in a research team. He is an organized and highly-motivated graduate student who can conduct his research with minimal guidance and is capable of facing new challenges. In addition, he is very polite with a pleasant personality.

Given the above facts, I believe that Paul will make great contributions to your research programs during his graduate studies. Therefore, I strongly recommend him for your graduate program. He deserves to be awarded any kind of assistantship, scholarship, or fellowship.

Sincerely yours,

Lucy Cole

Associate Professor, at University of xxx

Address:

Email:

48

To whom it may concern:

This recommendation letter has been written for Mr. John Thomas. I met John four years ago when I became the head of the xxx at the University of xxx. He is a very knowledgeable person in the field of computer engineering and so fond of his work. He does take the job seriously and uses all his knowledge along with his intelligence to solve the problems we face in our work. He is keen on learning new materials in the field of information technology.

In closing, I have enjoyed working with John and found him to be an intelligent and hardworking person with a very nice personality. Therefore, I strongly recommend him for your PhD program in xxx.

Please do not hesitate to contact me if you need further information.

Sincerely yours,

Aubree Woods

Faculty of xxx

49

July 14, 2012

To whom it may concern:

It is with pride that I recommend Mr. Tom Brand for admission to the xxx Scholarship program. In my capacity as a professor of Marketing at xxx University, I have worked closely with Tom for more than two years. He performed his master thesis under my supervision. During this course, I found him to be a very good student. Tom also was involved in several projects that we performed at the xxx Center. From these projects, I have found Tom to be a very capable person in analyzing and developing information systems. In addition, he is an enthusiastic researcher in the field of Computer Sciences and Information Technology.

Tom is an intelligent and hardworking person, and has shown to be successful in teamwork and independent work. It was a real honor to witness John's development here in our research center and it has been a joy to watch his growth since then. Therefore, I strongly recommend him for this scholarship program without any reservation.

Please do not hesitate to contact me if you need any further information.

Sincerely,

Kylie Ford

Head of Informatics Center

Faculty of Engineering

Email:

50

To whom it may concern:

This letter provides me the opportunity to recommend Ted Morris for admission to your Ph.D. program. I was familiar with Ted since he was an undergraduate student in our department. In his first year of graduate studies, he took two graduate courses with me. These courses were "xxx" and "xxx" in which he obtained admirable grades (3.87 and 3.73) as a result of his good performance in the exams and in the course projects. He painstakingly followed the issues of the coursework and tried to grow his domain of knowledge, particularly in the device area.

Ted has done his master thesis in xxx under my direct supervision, in which he has shown adaptability in working individually. Furthermore, his efforts resulted in three accepted papers in IEEE conferences.

Although he is an enthusiastic researcher in the field of xxx, he has experienced working in the fields of "xxx" and "xxx" for which he has passed some courses and audited the others. These courses have provided him with a background in all areas of Electronics.

I have found Ted to be an intelligent and hardworking student, capable of performing parallel tasks. He is an organized and highly-motivated graduate student who can conduct his projects and who is eager to face new challenges. In addition, he is polite and sociable with a nice personality.

Given the above facts, I believe that he will make great contributions to your research programs during his studies. Therefore, I strongly recommend him for your graduate program without any reservation. He deserves to be awarded any kind of assistantship, scholarship, or fellowship.

With my best regards,

Bella West, Ph.D.

Department of xxx

December 29, 2011

51

January 2, 2011

To whom it may concern:

This reference letter is provided at the request of Mr. Michael Doe, who has asked me to serve as a reference on his behalf. I have known him for more than a year as a graduate student in our department. He has taken two courses with me. These courses are "xxx" and "xxx" and Michael obtained the full grades in the courses as a result of his very best performances in various parts of the courses. Under my supervision, Michael has done his master thesis on "xxx".

From my interactions with Michael, I have found him to be an intelligent and hardworking student, capable of successfully cooperating in a research team. He is a self-motivated student who does perform his research with a minimal help and can come up with new ideas during his research activities. In addition, he is kind and polite with a nice personality. He is also organized and possesses high motivation for Ph.D. studies.

Given the above facts, I believe that Mr. Michael Doe will be a very successful graduate student, doing very well both in his courses and his research subjects assigned to him. Therefore, I strongly recommend him for your graduate program. He deserves to be awarded any kind of scholarship or fellowship.

Sincerely yours,

David Diaz

University of xxx

Email:

52

To whom it may concern:

It is a great pleasure for me to write this reference for Joe Johnson. I have known him since he started his M.Sc. degree in our department. In his second term, he took one of my graduate courses titled "xxx" and obtained the perfect grade in the course as a result of his good performance in the exams and in the course project. He is taking another course titled "xxx" with me this term.

Joe has a great ability in problem analysis, making him quite capable of facing new challenges. He is also an intelligent and hardworking person in research, while soft in social activities. He is successful in teamwork and independent work. He has presented several presentations in international conferences, which is a good indicator of his enthusiasm and motivation.

I believe Joe would perform competently with your program and has great potential, if challenged, to make a contribution to your field of study. I do recommend him for your Ph.D. program without any reservation.

Sincerely yours,

Prof. Jack Butler, Ph.D.

53

March 4, 2007

To whom it may concern:

This letter of recommendation has been written for Mr. Michael Larkin to attend your university for the graduate program in Business Studies. I have known him since fall 2001 as an undergraduate student in our department. He has taken MIS course with me obtaining an A as a result of a good performance in the exams and in the computer based assignments. Michael is a very talented student. He is intelligent, hardworking, and disciplined with a good personality. His English is well enough to make him capable of studying in an English environment without difficulty.

Michael continues to impress me with his knowledge, skill, and dedication to his work. I believe he exhibits many of the qualities that are essential to business students.

Given the above facts, I believe Mr. Michael Larkin will make very good accomplishments and contributions in your research groups. Therefore, I recommend this talented student unreservedly for graduate study in the field of his choice.

Sincerely yours,

Evan Powell

Department of xxx

Address:

Email:

54

To whom it may concern:

I would like to take an opportunity to offer a formal recommendation for William Fuller. I was asked to write as one who has functioned in the capacity of a research advisor of him. He has graduated from our department with an average of 3.8, the highest score in his more than 100 classmates. He has done his master thesis in xxx under my direct supervision.

Based on my interactions with William, I found him to be an intelligent, sincere, and hardworking person. He is capable of handling experimental and theoretical subjects. He also has an excellent ability to engage in teamwork. William is always consistent, dedicated and passionate, enthusiastic, and cheerful in his work, and a pleasure to work with. I feel confident that he will continue to succeed in his studies.

I sincerely recommend William as the ideal candidate for your graduate study. If you have any questions regarding this recommendation, please do not hesitate to contact me.

With best regards,

Eli Long, Professor of xxx at University of xxx

55

Williams Perry

0123 City Center

Way Berkeley, NY 94704

May 11, 2012

To whom it may concern:

It gives me immense pleasure in recommending Mr. John Park to attend your university for the Ph.D. program in Business Administration. I have known him for about four years as a graduate student in our department. He has taken xxx and xxx courses with me, obtaining good grades in both (3.7 and 3.82).

John has a total grade point average of 3.75, which is a good indication of his strong background in Business Studies. He has also been ranked the second among more than 120 students graduated in 2010 in our department.

In general, he is an intelligent and hardworking student capable of cooperating in a research team. He is very polite and disciplined with a pleasant personality. He is also fluent in English, both speaking and writing.

Given the above facts, I believe that John will make great contributions in your research groups and his graduate studies. Therefore, I strongly recommend him for your Ph.D. program. He deserves to be awarded any kind of financial aid.

Sincerely,

Prof. Williams Perry, Ph.D.

Dept. of xxx

Phone:

Email:

56

Subject: Recommendation Letter

February 07, 2010

To whom it may concern:

This letter of recommendation has been written for Mr. Richard Hanks to attend your Ph.D. program in Electronic Engineering. I have known him for more than a year in my capacity as a professor, department of Engineering. He has taken two graduate courses with me. He is also doing his M.Sc. thesis under my supervision.

After a year of working closely with him, I believe Richard has a strong background in his field of study. He is ranked first among his classmates, during his undergraduate studies, which indicates his high potential.

During his thesis, I found Richard to be a very hardworking, motivated, and committed student. He is purposeful and serious about his academic purpose and can conduct his research with a minimal guidance. In addition, Richard has a pleasant personality.

On the basis of the above, I strongly recommend him for your Ph.D. program and I am sure that he will perform very well during his study and become one of your best students.

Sincerely yours,

Gavin Ross, Professor of xxx

University of xxx

Email:

September 22, 2008

To whom it may concern:

It gives me great satisfaction to recommend a beloved student, Sara Salinger, for your graduate program. As her thesis supervisor for two years, I have watched this young woman develop both academically and personally into a mature individual, ready in every way for her graduate studies.

Sara is bright, energetic, compassionate, and genuinely well rounded. Her grades have been consistently above average in all of her courses. As per her performance records, she can be placed in the top 10% of a class of 90 students in our department. In addition, her project titled "xxx", conducted at xxx, was ranked among the best projects carried out in the department. She has shown the motivation, intelligence, preserving nature, and analytical aptitude for graduate study and research.

Considering all the above, I strongly recommend Sara for the graduate studies offered by your university, preferably with financial aid. If you have any questions regarding this recommendation, please do not hesitate to contact me.

Sincerely,

Audrey Kelly, Ph.D.

Email: xxx

58

To whom it may concern:

I am writing this letter of recommendation in support of Susan Fleming's application to the Ph.D. program at your university. I have known Susan for more than two years as a graduate student in our department. She finished her Master thesis under my supervision on xxx. In a short period, she presented outstanding research results. Her research endeavors have been published in several international conferences and prestigious journals.

Susan took two graduate courses, namely, "xxx" and "xxx", with me, obtaining excellent grades in the courses as a result of her outstanding performance. All of these are good indications of her high potential to be an excellent researcher.

In general, I have found Susan a hardworking, motivated, and committed student who can conduct her research with almost no guidance. She is fluent in the English language, both speaking and writing, in addition to her strong technical presentation skills. She has a polite, nice, and modest personality, which makes working with her very pleasant. I consider Susan to be one of the best students in our department and, in fact, she has been among the very best students I ever had during my tenure at the University of xxx.

In my opinion, Susan is a trustworthy individual and would be an excellent candidate for your program. Therefore, I strongly recommend her without any reservation. Please do not hesitate to contact me if you need further information.

Sincerely,

Alexis Wood

Professor of xxx at University of xxx

May 23, 2011

To whom it may concern:

I am very pleased to recommend George Brown for admission to your university program. I have known him since February 2007, when he started to work on his thesis under my supervision. His thesis subject was "xxx". George has finished his thesis successfully with an outstanding result (3.9).

During this course, I found George to be an enthusiastic researcher to elaborate conceptual ideas. His wide understanding of electronics concepts and his technical knowledge make him a successful Ph.D. student. In addition, he has a great ability in problem analysis, making him capable of facing new challenges. At the same time, he is very active in social life.

It was a real honor to witness George's development here at the university and it has been a joy to watch his growth since then. Therefore, I would, without reservation, recommend him to you. He would be a tremendous asset in your graduate program.

Sincerely,

Allison Gray

September 05, 2010

To whom it may concern:

This letter provides me the opportunity to recommend Mr. Bernard Villas to attend your university for the graduate program in Civil Engineering. I have known him for more than a year as a graduate student in our department. He has taken two courses with me, "xxx" and "xxx", obtaining the full grade of the course.

He has done several projects on "xxx" in groups of three and four members under my supervision. Because of their research efforts, the projects were successful and their results have published in prestigious journals in the field of xxx. Bernard's performance was brilliant in obtaining these outcomes.

I have found Bernard to be an intelligent and hardworking student, capable of cooperating in a research team. He can conduct his research with minimal guidance. He is also capable of facing new challenges, and finding good solutions to difficult problems in a timely manner. In addition, he is polite and disciplined with a nice personality. He is organized and possesses high motivation for graduate studies.

Given the above facts, I believe Bernard will make great contributions to your research programs during his graduate studies.

Therefore, I recommend him for your program. He deserves to be awarded any kind of assistantship, scholarship, or fellowship.

Sincerely yours,

Luke Ward

Address:

Email:

February 2, 2011

61

To whom it may concern:

It is a great pleasure for me to write this reference for Mr. Peter Treisi. I have known him for the last two years. He attended my xxx and xxx classes. During this course, he carried out a project under my direction and was among the top 2% students. I have also been his thesis advisor and I have seen that he demonstrated excellent research abilities while working on his thesis.

Through these experiences, I came to know him well. Peter is a brilliant scholar with a strong academic background. This is obvious from his very high GPA. He has intuitive solutions and shows intelligence and independence when working on his own or in teams.

I am sure that Peter, with his outstanding personal characteristics and research abilities, will be successful in any academic endeavor. He has certainly demonstrated the necessary skills to make a fine researcher. Therefore, I strongly recommend him for graduate study and research assistantship in any computer science program.

Yours sincerely,

Anna Ramirez, Ph.D.

To whom it may concern:

I am writing to you in support of Tom Doe and his desire to attend the University of xxx for the PhD program in xxx. I have known him for the last two years. He attended my xxx and xxx classes. For these courses, he carried out several projects under my direction and was among the top 2% of students.

Based on my interactions with Tom during the course I taught and during his research activities, I found him to be an intelligent, sincere, hardworking, and innovative person with the ability to engage in teamwork.

I am sure that Tom, with his outstanding personal characteristics and research abilities, will be successful in any academic endeavor. He has certainly demonstrated the necessary skills to make an excellent researcher. Therefore, I strongly recommend him for graduate study and research assistantship in any electrical engineering program.

With best regards,

Zoe Nelson

Address:

To whom it may concern:

I would like to take an opportunity to offer a formal recommendation for Jack Glass. He has been my student for several years. He is interested in continuing his studies toward a PhD degree in Accounting and I feel that he would be an excellent candidate for your esteemed program.

From the research and academic point of view, I see Jack as a talented student who is capable of reaching higher levels of education in his field of study. He is organized and possesses high motivation for graduate studies.

Jack gained the top score in my classes and participated very well in the class discussions and group projects. He was also ranked second in the university entrance exam, which is a good indication of his capabilities.

Considering all the above, I recommend Jack for your graduate studies. If you have any questions regarding this recommendation, please contact me.

Best regards,

Mason King, professor of xxx at xxx

To whom it may concern:

This is to certify that Ms. Martha Hajson is a graduate student in the Department of Electrical and Computer Engineering at xxx University. Martha has been my student in the Electronics course. During this course, she proved herself to be a very good student with regular attendance in the class and being an active participant in discussions. She is a pleasant, hardworking, and reliable person to work with.

I feel confident Martha will continue to succeed in her studies. She is a dedicated student and thus far, her grades have been exemplary. Martha is always passionate and enthusiastic in her work, and a pleasure to work with.

It is for these reasons that I offer high recommendations for her without reservation.

Sincerely,

Victoria Green

Address:

February 22, 2008

65

To whom it may concern:

It gives me immense pleasure in recommending Mr. Michael Lee for the graduate program in Computer Science at your university. I have known him since he was a graduate student in our department. During his M.Sc. study, he took my graduate course in "xxx" and obtained 3.9 score as a result of a good performance in the exams and in the course project. Michael performed comprehensive research on the xxx in our newborn laboratory for his master thesis, Michael was also responsible for installing the workstations and related software tools.

Even though he has been an active researcher in the field of xxx, he has taken several courses in Physics and Operation of Semiconductor Devices. This has provided him with a strong background in all areas of electronics.

Michael is successful in teamwork and independent work and has been an active member in organizing conferences, seminars, and workshops in our research center. I recommend him for your Ph.D. program without reservation. He deserves to be awarded any kind of assistantship or fellowship.

Sincerely,

June 23, 2011

To whom it may concern:

As a professor of Management in the department of Business and Management Studies at xxx University, I am delighted to recommend a talented student of our graduate program, Tom Brown, to your PhD program in Finance. I write this letter on his behalf.

I have known Tom since 2008, second semester as a graduate student in our department. He has taken xxx course with me obtaining 3.8 as a result of a good performance in the exams and the assignments. This becomes more significant when you may notice that he ranked second in his class of about 50 students. He also accomplished his final course project about amplifiers with feedback successfully.

Tom is a clever and hardworking student. His high GPA is a good indicator of his academic capabilities. It should be mentioned that he was always among the top five students in our department during his study. In addition, his English is proficient, in both written and spoken, to make him capable of studying in an English environment without any difficulty.

Given the above facts, I believe that Tom will make great contributions in your research groups. Therefore, I strongly recommend him for your graduate program.

Sincerely yours,

Lauren Hill

Address:

January 02, 2010

67

March 1, 2007

To whom it may concern:

I am writing this letter of recommendation in support of Mr. Ted Williams, a B.Sc. student of our department, the applicant to your graduate program. I have known him for more than two years. He has been my student in the course "xxx", in which the result has been very good (Mark A).

Ted is a very hardworking, intelligent, polite, and serious person. He has a fundamental knowledge in core courses of Electrical Engineering and Mathematics required for continuing his studies. He also has some practical experiences in the field, which will help him doing independent research projects.

Therefore, I wholeheartedly recommend Ted to your graduate program and I am sure that he will be an outstanding candidate.

Sincerely,

James Wright

University of xxx

68

Subject: Letter of Recommendation

Bella Allen

1234 State University Drive

 Los Angeles, CA 90032-8530

Phone Number: (323) 343-3000

To whom it may concern:

I have had the pleasure of having Peter Jordan as a graduate student in my classes and my research team for three years at xxx Business School. During this course, Peter has been more than the ideal student. To achieve the highest grades and my deepest respect, he has proven outstanding performance and maintained a clear sense of purpose.

Peter's astuteness and hardworking characteristics helped him gain precious experiences and knowledge within his studies. His achievement in keeping his GPA high is an important aspect of his studies. He has always kept himself among the top 5% of the class of 2009.

I also would like to mention Peter's originality in the work and his analytical ability and clearance in judgment. His English proficiency in both written and oral expression makes him able to study in an English environment and work in international research projects.

Based on his personal and educational background, I recommend him for any graduate education in Electrical Engineering and related areas without reservation.

Sincerely,

Bella Allen

Email:

April 3, 2010

To whom it may concern:

This letter of recommendation has been written for Joe Peterson to attend your university for the graduate program. I have known him since 2001, second semester as an undergraduate student in our department. He has taken xxx course with me, obtaining 3.8 as a result of a good performance in the exams and in the computer based assignments. This becomes more significant when you may notice that he ranked second in his class of about 50 students. He also accomplished his final course project about xxx successfully with feedback.

Joe was always among the top three students in our department during his study. He is a talented and hardworking student. In addition, he is disciplined with a good personality.

Given the above facts, I believe Joe will make great contributions in your research groups. Therefore, I strongly recommend him for your graduate program. He deserves to be awarded any kind of assistantship and/or scholarship.

Sincerely yours,

Prof. Jill Williams

To whom it may concern:

This is a letter of reference in support of Mr. John Lopes, the applicant to your graduate studies program. I have known him for about three years, from the time he was my student in xxx course, which was taught entirely in English, with an outstanding performance.

John also took the xxx course with me, in which he was ranked first in his class, among more than 50 students. His hardworking characteristics make him capable of gaining excellent working experiences within his studies.

John's brilliant achievement in keeping his GPA significantly high during his studies is a good indicator of his academic and research capabilities.

I also would like to mention his analytical ability, which makes him an excellent candidate for graduate study in xxx.

Based on his personal and educational background, I have to recommend him for any graduate education in Civil Engineering without reservation.

Sincerely,

Prof. John Peterson

71

March 19, 2007

To the committee of admissions:

This letter is in support of Bill Richland's application to the Business School of xxx Accounting program. I have known Bill for the last four years and have had various opportunities to assess his performance both in my capacity as an instructor and a supervisor.

As instructor, I noticed that he was an enthusiastic learner. Bill ranked in the top 5% of his class throughout his academic career. He fulfilled all the requirements with the added challenge of honors and advanced courses. He is intelligent, inquisitive, and yearns to gain an in-depth knowledge. With his determination and hard work, I have no doubt that he will succeed in all his endeavors.

As a supervisor, I mentored Bill through a project on xxx. He has developed a comprehensive framework to assess key factors influencing the adoption of new technology. While being thorough and meticulous in his work, I noticed that he was also extremely quick in his evaluation and action.

In my personal interaction with Bill, I found him to be highly suitable for a graduate program in business studies. Naturally, I was glad to hear that it was his chosen field of future opportunity.

In closing, it is with sincere conviction that I enthusiastically and very strongly recommend Bill for admission to your program on his outstanding merit.

Sincerely,

Sophie Lee

Professor of xxx at the university of xxx

To whom it may concern:

Frank Salinger has been my student over the entire four-year period of his undergraduate education. He had several courses with me in MIS, Research Methods, and Information systems, and I would like to recommend him as an ideal candidate for your program. Frank was selected for our program with a ranking of second among 800 applicants.

Throughout his educational period, he has distinguished himself academically and otherwise. He was always ranked within the top 1% of his class. His high GPA demonstrates his strong academic background.

Frank is a pleasant young man with a good sense of humor. His communication skills and sense of planning and management are among the best I have seen. He is very well suited for a PhD program in business studies and I am sure your program will find a worthy candidate in him. Therefore, I take this opportunity to recommend Frank to your program.

I will be available to provide email and number for any further queries you may have on Frank's application.

Sincerely,

To whom it may concern:

This reference letter is provided at the request of Mr. James Morgan, who has asked me to serve as a reference on his behalf. The information contained in this letter is confidential and should be treated as such. The information should not be disclosed to anyone who would not be involved in the admission decision regarding this individual.

James worked on his thesis under my direct supervision during the last 18 months. As his supervisor, I have had an opportunity to observe his research endeavors. I would rate James' overall performance in this project as outstanding. He was a brilliant student with a passion for technology and its management. He always ranked within the top 1% of his class across all streams and won much recognition for his department through useful, practical research in the field of xxx.

I understand that you are looking for students who are motivated and excel in their academic and research backgrounds, and therefore feel that your program would be a perfect match for James.

I recommend James with a sense of pride and satisfaction in how he has turned out and assure you that he will make outstanding contributions to your school. Please feel free to contact me in reference to this letter.

Sincerely,

Prof. Davis Ashley, Ph.D.

Professor of xxx

To whom it may concern:

I have known Mr. Ahamd Moshfegh for about four years as an undergraduate student in our department. He took my HRM course, where he obtained the highest grade in the course (3.85).

Because his strong background in his field of study and his hardworking character, I am sure that he will continue his graduate studies with great success. In fact, his ranking among his classmates is a good indication of the depth of learning and a good proof of his high potentials and capabilities. Comparing him with other undergraduate students of our department in the past four years, I can rank him among the top 5%.

Ahmad is an intelligent and hardworking student with a pleasant personality. He has the ability to work independently and to active;y participate in research teams.

Given the above facts, I believe that he will make significant accomplishments and contributions in your graduate studies. He deserves to be awarded any kind of assistantship, scholarship, or fellowship.

Sincerely,

To whom it may concern:

It is a pleasure to recommend Fred Lowe for graduate studies in the field of Industrial Engineering. Fred was admitted to our undergraduate program at the xxx University in 2008. As of now, he has successfully taken all coursework and has maintained a GPA of 3.85. That incredibly high grade ranks Fred at the top of his class. I should confess that being the top ranked student in our university takes a lot of talent and hard work. He currently is working on his Master Thesis and he is expected to finish it at the end of this term.

Fred has taken several courses with me and has earned good grades in all of them. In the xxx course, he demonstrated his ability in systematic thinking by putting up an innovative production system in xxx. He went on to make a perfect grade (4) in the course. His performance in my classes is indicative of his interest in the subject matter and his dedication to his chosen field of study.

Because of his academic capabilities, Fred has been invited to participate in several research projects in different areas of Business and Management. He has also taken up an MIS project to survey the Social Security System. A summarized version of the latter has been published in high ranked Journals of Management.

Fred has also worked as a TA in our department for almost a year. He was responsible for conducting problem-solving sessions for "MIS" course, administering quizzes, and grading. He has performed his assignment with utmost degree of enthusiasm and professionalism. Since July 2009, Fred has worked as a part-time consultant on different projects in MIS and Operations Research.

Fred is a mature student with a pleasant personality. He works well in a team and yet his judgment can be trusted to meet the objectives in individual efforts. His qualification motivates me to recommend him for graduate studies without reservation. I do believe that he will be eminently successful as a graduate student.

Sincerely,

Eli Brown

Associate Prof. Peter Richardson

Department of xxx

76

April 16, 2009

To whom it may concern:

I would like to take an opportunity to offer a formal recommendation for Mr. Jack Hanks to attend your university for the graduate program. I have known him for more than a year as an undergraduate student in our department. He took one course, Electronics, with me and he obtained 3.9 score as a result of his excellent performance in various parts of the course, including exams, homework assignments, and class discussions. He has ranked first in a class of about 50 students. Jack is a very talented student with the potential to become a brilliant graduate student.

From my interactions with him, I have found Jack to be an intelligent and hardworking student. I anticipate that he will be capable of successfully cooperating in a research team. He is a self-motivated student who perform his tasks without help. Furthermore, Jack is very kind, polite, and disciplined. He has a nice and modest personality. He also has high motivation to continue his graduate studies.

Given the above facts, I strongly recommend him for your graduate program. He deserves to be awarded any kind of assistantship, scholarship, or fellowship. Please do not hesitate to contact me if you have any questions.

Sincerely,

Taylor Miller

77

December 20, 2011

To whom it may concern:

This letter of recommendation has been written in support of Mr. Ali Keshavarz's application for admission to your graduate program. I have known Ali for almost two years. During his undergraduate studies at the University of xxx, he took two courses with me, xxx and xxx, in which he was one of my best students. He was also involved in some educational activities. He worked as a Teaching Assistant (TA) in several courses under my supervision. His quality in giving guidance to the students and helping them was outstanding. His research potential was also very high in working in a team where he proved to be a creative person.

Ali is a hardworking, persistent, and intelligent student. His merits are well reflected by his GPA, which is the top among his fellow students. In addition, His English proficiency is good in both written and spoken and I think he will have no problem in an English environment.

I am sure that with his personal characteristics and educational record, Ali will be successful in any academic endeavor. Therefore,

I recommend him for graduate study and any kind of financial assistantship.

Sincerely,

Evan Jones

To whom it may concern:

This letter is in support of Brian Holms for applying to graduate studies in your department. I had the opportunity to work with this young and talented student as his thesis supervisor for last 15 months. During this course, I have found him a brilliant researcher with an exceptional capacity for analytical thinking.

Brian has been a top student during his graduate studies. In fact, his academic performance during this time was excellent. His high GPA is a good indicator of his strong background. I believe that Brian exhibits many of the qualities that are essential to business students. I have seen many examples of his talent and have long been impressed by his diligence and work ethic.

As such, I strongly recommend him to continue his graduate studies in your department and wish him a successful career in the future.

Sincerely,

Sarah Moore

January 4, 2009

To whom it may concern:

It is a pleasure to recommend Mr. Paul Kings for your PhD program in the field of management. I have known Paul since he entered our graduate program in MIS. He was ranked second in our entrance exam and this gave him the opportunity to continue his study in this challenging program.

As his advisor at xxx University, I have found this talented student to be a multifaceted person with strong academic and research background. He is distinguished for a number of important achievements during his study in our department. For one thing, he has ranked first among his classmates with an outstanding GPA (3.92).

In the second Engineering Conference held in xxx, the article presented by Paul was recognized as the best all-around work. Aside from his extracurricular activities, Paul has also been successful in intramural athletics. He has been a member of our chess team during his studies in our university.

Considering all the facts, I recommend Paul for your program without reservation and I believe that he will be eminently successful in his future academic endeavors.

Sincerely,

Prof. Alyssa Smith, Ph.D.

March 3, 2010

To whom it may concern:

This is to certify that Mr. Pooria Akbari is a senior student in our Computer Engineering department. I have known Pooria for about four years. He has taken several courses with me and I can say that he is a talented and hardworking student. His records as a Teaching Assistant (TA) and his willingness for further studies show his qualifications for original work and research. His interests include xxx and related areas in which he is strongly recommended as a graduate applicant. I feel confident of his potential in pursuing his studies.

In short, I can assure you of his competence for research in his proposed field of study, and recommend you to carefully assess his application. If you have any further question regarding this recommendation, please feel free to contact me.

Sincerely,

Claire White

To whom it may concern:

It is my honor to recommend Gary Owen to your graduate program. I first got to know Gary at the annual conference in Business and Management. Because of his quantitative perspective and critical vision, which impressed me immediately, I encouraged him to apply to our graduate program in Marketing. Fortunately, he was interested in this program and we had the chance to have him here in our department for last two years.

I also served as Gary's thesis supervisor on xxx. Through daily communications and discussions on his research project, I find that Gary is very diligent and self-motivated in research work. Keeping an open and active mind, he keeps himself well informed with every breakthrough in his field of study. As a graduate student, Gary has demonstrated a great capacity and adaptability in scientific research. His strong mathematical background contributed impressively to his search endeavors.

Gary is also good at technical writing in English. He has co-authored two book chapters with me. He is an active member of student society and often volunteers his help wherever needed, such as delivering monthly newsletters and preparing for the seminars.

As a professor of Marketing at xxx University, I can assure you that Gary has well prepared for his quest for academic achievements of the highest order. Without reservation, I give my highest recommendations for him to your Ph.D. program.

Sincerely yours,

Prof. Joe Rickard

September 01, 2011

82

Gavin Jackson

123 Golden Shore,

Long Beach, **CA** 90802

Tel: (562) 951-4000

February 01, 2012

To whom it may concern:

I am proud to recommend a beloved student, Ahmad Montazeri. I have known him for the last two years. He attended my xxx class. In this course, he carried out a project under my direction and was among the top 2% students. I have also been his advisor during his internship, where he demonstrated excellent research abilities while working on a project.

Through these experiences, I came to know him well. Ahmad is a very good student and this is obvious from his GPA. He has intuitive solutions and shows intelligence and independence when working on his own or in teams.

Ahmad is calm and very polite. He interacts well with other students and the staff of the university. He communicates well in Farsi or

English in both informal and seminar settings. He has sound logic and well-ordered points to make.

I am sure that Ahmad, with his outstanding personal characteristics and research abilities, will be successful in any academic endeavor. He has certainly demonstrated the necessary skills to make a fine researcher. Therefore, I recommend him for graduate study and research assistantship in any computer science program.

Yours sincerely,

Gavin Jackson

To whom it may concern:

I have had the distinct pleasure to recommend Mr. Richard Stone to your graduate program in Mathematics. I have known Richard for two years. During this time, I have had him in one of my courses, namely "xxx". Richard's outstanding performance in this class convinces me to write this recommendation. I believe that he is an excellent student and a brilliant researcher.

In addition to his exceptional academic records, Richard has been an active member of student affairs during his study at xxx University. During this time, he has participated in many student activities. Therefore, students have elected him as a member of the Student Council for the second time.

Considering all the facts, I believe Richard is well qualified to continue his studies toward a PhD. degree in Mathematics and related areas and I recommend him for graduate studies and research assistantship in your university. If you have any question regarding this recommendation, please do not hesitate to contact me.

Sincerely,

Jack Richardson

June 23, 2009

To whom it may concern:

It is a pleasure for me to write this reference letter for Peter Flester. I came to know him two years ago when he completed the course "xxx" taught by me at Electrical Engineering department. During this course, although there were many high-level students in the class, most good questions and discussions came from him. His outstanding performance helped him to pass the course with an exceptional grade.

Peter had another course with me on "xxx" last semester and passed it with a grade of 3.8, which was the second highest grade in the class. During this time, I came to know him well. He is a brilliant and hardworking student who has shown intelligence, independence, and a sound knowledge during his studies. Peter has a likable personality and interacts well with other students.

Given Peter's research capabilities as a student and outstanding character as a person, I am sure he will be successful in any academic endeavor. He has certainly demonstrated the necessary skills to become a brilliant researcher. Therefore, I strongly recommend him for graduate studies in Electrical Engineering. I believe he absolutely deserves any kind of fellowship or assistantship.

Sincerely yours,

Henry Thomas

Professor of xxx at xxx

To whom it may concern:

I have known Laura Davis for about four years as an undergraduate student in our Department. She has participated in my two courses, obtaining very good grades. Because of her strong background in her field of study, her interest in xxx, and her hardworking characteristic, I am sure that she will continue her graduate studies with great success.

Laura has a pleasant personality. She is very polite and disciplined with the ability to work independently or in a team. Her sensitivity, diligence, energy, and sense of humor made working with her a joy.

Given the above facts, I rank her among top 10% students and believe she will make significant contributions to your program. She deserves to be awarded any kind of assistantship, scholarship, or fellowship. Therefore, I strongly recommend this lovely young woman for your graduate program.

Sincerely,

Prof. Sarah Harris, Ph.D.

February 06, 2008

To whom it may concern:

I am privileged to write in support of my dear friend and student, Jessica Walton. She studied in my classroom two years. During this course, I witnessed her tremendous growth and development in both academic achievement and character.

To begin with, Jessica is an exceptional student with a strong academic background in Management studies. Her high GPA is a true indicator of her capabilities. The academics in our department are challenging and Jessica fulfilled all the requirements with outstanding performance. She has excellent written and verbal communication skills, is organized, and can work independently.

In regard to her personality, one has only to speak to her to recognize her openness and eagerness. Jessica is exceptionally diligent and hardworking. She is exceptionally considerate and sensitive. She is not only good humored and friendly, but is also good at gauging other people's level of knowledge and attitudes.

Overall, I believe Jessica has a very bright future and I am sure that she would benefit from your graduate program. Therefore, I give her my highest recommendation, and very much hope that you judge her application favorably.

Sincerely,

Jack Scott

Address:

Email:

Tel:

87

Date: 09/11/2010

To whom it may concern:

I am happy to write a letter of recommendation for a talented student, Helen Garcia, in support of her application to the Department of Physics' program. She took the classroom version of xxx this past fall. Based on her performance in the course, I feel she would be a good candidate for the xxx program. Grading in my courses is based on a combination of objective and subjective evaluations.

The objective components are homework and open-book examinations. The more subjective component is participation in small group discussions about case studies based on articles. Helen's overall grade in the course was outstanding and put her among 1% of the students.

I was also Helen's direct thesis supervisor. Her project's focus of interest was quantum. Our department is the ideal place to carry out such research, and this helped Helen to put her brilliant ideas into practice. I am sure that her discoveries will make an impact on learning in that field in the future.

I regard Helen's academic and research abilities as excellent. Therefore, I strongly recommend her for graduate study at xxx.

Yours sincerely,

David Hill

Department of xxx

88

LETTER OF RECOMENDATION

April 08, 2012

Applicant: Barbara Thomas

Recommender: Prof. Daniel Wilson

To whom it may concern:

At the request of Barbara Thomas, who is currently applying to your university for embarking on a degree program in Electronics Engineering, I am happy to compose this letter of reference on her behalf. I have known Barbara since September 2009; being a graduate student, she attended my lectures on xxx, and on xxx. During this course, she demonstrated herself as an active and hardworking student. With a keen craving for new knowledge, Barbara was most attentive in my classes and always provided insightful questions and discussions to me. Her papers and her classroom performance are all a distinct manifestation of her wonderful analytical skills, careful logic, and her quick-witted thinking.

As her teacher, I am proud of Barbara for her academic achievements. She certainly stands out as a student of great potential. She is already a seasoned expert in both Electronics and Computer Science at this young age. If you give her a chance to continue her study at your esteemed university, I have no doubt that Barbara will take full advantage of this precious opportunity to make herself a first-rate scholar.

Should you make further inquiries concerning Barbara Thomas, please do not hesitate to contact me.

Sincerely,

Prof. Daniel Wilson

Professor of xxx

89

Levi Evans

111 Campus Street

Loma Linda, CA 92354

March 07, 2011

To whom it may concern:

I consider it a great pleasure and a responsibility to recommend to Sharon Hall as a worthy candidate for your graduate program in Sociology. As a professor of Sociology at the department of xxx, I deliver different courses in related areas. I came to know Sharon when she was a freshman, thus I have an overall understanding of her.

She took my courses in xxx and xxx and obtained the perfect grades as a result of an outstanding performance in her exams and in the course projects. I have also served as Sharon's thesis supervisor. Because of her strong academic background, Sharon was able to carry out her research in a timely manner and with great results.

After these years of working with her, I believe Sharon has a good attitude and is capable of working in a group and acting independently. I can say that she is the best student among the ones I had supervised for in past years.

Seeing her serious yearning for further education, I think that it will be very beneficial for both xxx University and Sharon to continue her education in your graduate program. Therefore, I strongly recommend her for admission.

Sincerely,

Levi Evans

Email:

90

Subject: A recommendation letter for Ruth Lewis

Claire Nelson

Address:

Email:

Tel:

To whom it may concern:

I think extremely highly of Ruth Lewis, who is interested in your MBA program. Therefore, it is my great pleasure to write a letter of recommendation on her behalf. I have known Ruth for more than two years. She took two courses with me: Research methodology and Accounting and she got high grades in all of them as a result of her outstanding performance.

During this course, I consider Ruth to be one of the most intelligent students I have had in our department. She is very precise. She is a deep thinker and quite innovative in finding solutions to new problems she faces. In addition to her excellent academic capabilities, she has shown strong communication and social capabilities. I enjoyed having her in my class.

Given her talents and interests, she is well prepared to enter into an MBA program. I strongly recommend her and I am sure she will be able to satisfy a high educational standard at the graduate level very well.

Sincerely yours,

Claire Nelson

Associate professor of xxx

91

Subject: A recommendation letter for Angela Lopez

January 03, 2012

To whom it may concern:

I am a professor at xxx Medical University of xxx, and was Angela Lopez's advisor for her graduation thesis. She asked me to recommend her for admission to your PhD program. I am pleased to write on her behalf. I have known her for more than two years as a graduate student in our department.

During her thesis research, Angela gained valuable experience working with equipment of xxx. I should emphasize here that she is very accurate and diligent in her experimental work and in treating the results. Working closely with Angela, I found her an exceptional student with a solid educational background and a remarkable ability in lab experimental. In addition, she has an excellent command of English.

Overall, her academic background will ensure her remarkable success in her future studies. Therefore, I recommend her enthusiastically.

Sincerely yours,

Camilla Rogers

Professor of xxx

92

April 11, 2010

To whom it may concern:

As a director at University of xxx, I deem it a pleasure to recommend Amy Scott, one of the outstanding students in our department, for admission and assistantship to your graduate program.

As her teacher and former advisor, I am proud of Amy for her academic achievements. She certainly stands out as a student of great potential. Comparing her with other students of our department in the past four years, I can rank her among the top 2%.

Professionally and ethically, Amy has proven herself to be a highly qualified researcher. She has a good attitude and capable of working in a group and acting independently. Amy is also active in daily life. Drawing pictures well, she is optimistic and always ready to offer help.

Amy is very likeable and ambitious person. I have no doubt that she will be a serious and enthusiastic student, and someday a quite successful researcher that you would be proud to call an alumni.

Please feel free to call (xxx) or write (xxx@xxx.edu) if I can be helpful.

Sincerely,

Evan Perez

93

To whom it may concern:

This letter is written to recommend Janet Perez for M.S. program at your university. I have known her for more than two years. She has taken two of my undergraduate courses, namely, xxx and xxx, in which she obtained grades 3.7 and 3.8 respectively, and ranked among top 5% of her class.

Janet has a strong background in the basic courses of Engineering. She has a total grade point average of 3.7, which is a good indication of her learning and deep understanding of almost all courses and her potential to continue her graduate studies. She has obtained the third highest ranking among more than 120 students graduated in 2009 in our Department of xxx. In fact, she had the chance to continue her graduate studies in our department, but she is willing to participate in your graduate program.

Janet is a very intelligent and hardworking student. She is capable of cooperating in a research team work. Personally, she is a polite and pleasant person to work with. In addition, she is fluent in English, both in writing and speaking.

I strongly recommend her, and believe that she deserves to be awarded a scholarship or research/teaching assistantship. I am very confident that she will achieve a great success in her future research and study endeavors.

Sincerely yours

David Bell, Associate Professor of xxx

94

Dear Colleagues:

I am happy to write a letter of recommendation for Lory Reed in support of her application to your graduate program in Finance. I have known her for more than two years. She has participated in my xxx and xxx courses. In these courses, she had outstanding results (3.9 and 3.85), as a result of her eagerness and seriousness. She showed herself to be an active and hardworking student.

Lory has some of the best qualities of a researcher. I would describe her as having a solid academic background in the field of xxx. She is very polite and disciplined. She has also the ability to work independently.

Because of her hardworking character, I am sure that she will continue her graduate studies with great success. Given the above facts, I believe that she will make significant contributions to your graduate program.

Sincerely,

Prof. Robert James, Ph.D.

February 2, 2010

To whom it may concern:

I am pleased to write on behalf of Judy Moris. She asked me to recommend her for admission to the University of Delaware's graduate program in HRM. I have known Judy for more than two years. She has been my student in the "Human Resource Management" course, in which her result was outstanding, obtaining 3.8. She always actively participated in discussions throughout the course. In addition, she had an excellent final project about the role of e-HRM in enhancing employees' performance.

During this course, July was also an active student in university life. She is a member of student associations and was an active organizer of student affairs. Personally, she is a well-organized, intelligent, and hardworking person.

Regarding the above, I recommend Judy for any graduate studies in HRM areas without reservation. Please feel free to contact me if you need further information.

Sincerely,

Aaron Thomas

To whom it may concern:

I am privileged to write in support of a talented student, Tracy Burke, who is applying to the Ph.D. program at your university. I have known her for more than a year, having been her Mathematics lecturer. Because of her dutiful attitude towards school, her brilliant ideas, and pleasant personality, she is one of my favorite students.

Tracy is a hardworking girl. Her high grades are definitely a result of her own endeavors and efforts. She is able to work under tremendous pressure and meet deadlines. Teachers and students often remark that Tracy is blessed with considerable talent. In our department, everyone sees how hard she works to cultivate her talent in both her academics and outdoor activities.

I can assure you that admitting Tracy will not be a mistake. I am confident that she will work extra hard and earn her degree in a record time.

Sincerely,

David Lynch

March 9, 2009

To whom it may concern:

It is with the utmost pleasure and honor that I recommend Sadie Silva for your graduate program in Information Systems. As her direct thesis supervisor, I have found her to be a hardworking, motivated, and talented student. In fact, Sadie has been more than the ideal student. To achieve the highest grade and my deepest respect, she has demonstrated outstanding performance in her research project.

Sadie has a strong background in her field of study. Her high GPA puts her at the top of her class. She also has published several papers in international conferences and prestigious journals. These all are good indications of her high potentials to become an excellent researcher.

I will always hold her in the highest esteem, I sincerely recommend Sadie Silva as the ideal candidate for your graduate program. I recommend you to consider her application carefully. Please do not hesitate to contact me if you need more information about this recommendation or Sadie.

Sincerely,

Prof. John Day, University of xxx

December 2, 2011

To whom it may concern:

I am writing this letter of recommendation in support of Mable Neal's application to your Ph.D. Program in Accounting. I have known her since her enrollment in our department as a graduate student. Mable has taken two graduate courses with me, namely xxx and xxx, in which she gained excellent grades of 3.7 and 3.75, respectively.

During this course, I found that Mable is deeply attracted to her field of study and she follows her study with a great interest. She has a consistent, challenging, and socially mature characteristics. She is intelligent, creative, and hardworking with a strong background in xxx while being quite familiar with research techniques. I believe she is a valuable member of every researching team, especially in the field of Accounting.

I strongly recommend her for your program and wish her success in her future academic career.

Sincerely,

Richard Jensen

To whom it may concern:

I highly recommend Diana Davidson as a candidate for your graduate program. I have known Diana for 15 months, having been her direct thesis supervisor. During this time, I have found her to be a very hardworking young woman. Her outstanding performance in her research thesis on e-Business urged me to write this reference letter on her behalf.

Diana is a diligent, quick learner with an exceptionally strong academic background. She is a deep thinker and a motivated researcher in the field of IT Management. Her results in both undergraduate and graduate studies are a good indicator of her capabilities.

Diana's energy and sense of humor made working with her a joy. Therefore, I recommend her as a welcome addition to the program. Please do not hesitate to contact me if you have any question regarding this recommendation or Diana's application.

Sincerely,

Prof. Andro Kari, Department of xxx

100

To whom it may concern:

This letter of recommendation is in support of Mona Obrien's application for the admission into your Ph.D. program. I have known her since she became an employee at xxx company. She has been working in Engineering Department for about four years and she has been participating in several projects such as xxx and xxx.

During this time, I have found Mona to be an intelligent employee who is capable of cooperating in a research team. She is capable of facing new challenges and finding good solutions for difficult problems. She is organized and possesses high motivation for graduate studies. In addition, she is very polite and disciplined with a nice personality. I enjoy working with her in our research group.

Given the above facts, I believe Mona will make great contributions to your research programs during her graduate studies and therefore strongly recommend her. She deserves to be awarded any kind of assistantship or fellowship.

Sincerely yours,

Dr. Mark Soto

Made in United States
Orlando, FL
26 January 2025

57850659R00104